Words for a Journey

The Art of Being with Dementia

Pattern Language 3.0 Catalogue Series

Learning Patterns: A Pattern Language for Creative Learning

Presentation Patterns: A Pattern Language for Creative Presentation

Collaboration Patterns: A Pattern Language for Creative Collaborations

Words for a Journey: The Art of Being with Dementia

Survival Language: A Pattern Language for Surviving Earthquakes

Change Making Patterns: A Pattern Language for Fostering Social Entrepreneurship

Words for a Journey
The Art of Being with Dementia

Takashi Iba and Makoto Okada
with
Iba Laboratory & Dementia Friendly Japan Initiative

Copyright © 2015 by Takashi Iba, Makoto Okada, Iba Laboratory, and Dementia Friendly Japan Initiative

All rights reserved. This book or any portion thereof may not be reproduced or used in any manner whatsoever without the express written permission of the publisher except for the use of brief quotations in a book review or scholarly journal.

The authors and publisher have taken care in the preparation of this book, but no liability is assumed for incidental or consequential damages in connection with or arising out of the use of the information contained herein.

First Printing: 2015
V.1.00

ISBN 978-1-312-73484-5

CreativeShift Lab, Inc.
Mizunobu Bldg., 7F, Kitasaiwai 1-11-1, Nishi Ward,
Yokohama, Kanagawa, Japan zip 220-0004
www.creativeshiftlab.com

Words for a Jouenry Project
Iba Laboratory, Keio University: Takashi Iba, Aya Matsumoto, Arisa Kamada, Nao Tamaki, Tasuku Matsumura, Tomoki Kaneko, with Taichi Isaku

Dementia Friendly Japan Initiative (DFJI): Makoto Okada (Fujitsu Laboratories Ltd.), Takehito Tokuda (Dementia Friendship Club), Katsuaki Tanaka (KOKUYO S&T Co., Ltd.), Masahiko Shoji (Center for Global Communications, International University of Japan), Yasufumi Okui and Tsutomu Ikezawa (Dai Nippon Printing Co., Ltd.)

Illustrations by Arisa Kamada, Tasuku Matsumura, and Takashi Iba
Cover Design by Aya Matsumoto

Toward a dementia-friendly society

Preface

Dementia is something we all should be familiar with. Of the elderly people over 65 years of age in Japan, including those with mild symptoms, over 8 million have Dementia. These statistics reveal that 1 in 4 elderly or 1 in 15 Japanese overall have dementia. If you walk through any given neighborhood, chances are high that many of them contain dementia patients and family members who care for them. Now, you should have an idea of how close everyone is to the disease.

There are many with dementia who are living well. They have not given up everything in their lives just because they have the disease. It is a fact that you will have to make some changes in your lifestyle once you have been diagnosed with dementia; but try looking at it this way: if you are going to have to make changes, why not make good ones? Think of it as the start of a new journey: a journey to live well with dementia. By spending more time with your family, you will get to know them even better. The time that is approaching is not a time to lose what you have, but a time to gain even more. How you spend this time is completely up to you and your family.

This book contains 40 "words" that will come in handy for living well with dementia. These words have been constructed as the result of interviews with dementia patients, their families, and people who support the cause.

The 40 words in the book are called "Words for a Journey," because our hope is that dementia patients and the people around them will use the words as guides to the adventure of living well with dementia. Look through the words and to find hints for your journey.

Contents

Preface — vii

About This Book — xiv

How to Read — xvi

How to Use — xviii

WORDS FOR A JOURNEY — 1

WORDS FOR THE CARED — 5

WORDS FOR THE CARING — 35

WORDS FOR EVERYONE — 71

The Journey Continues … — 89

Utilizing Words for a Journey: Ideas for Every Stakeholder — 90

Afterword — 92

Acknowledgements — 94

References — 95

[WORDS FOR A JOURNEY]

1. A New Journey

----- 2

WORDS FOR THE CARED

6. Can-Do List

----- 14

11. Turning the Tide

----- 24

2. The First Step

----- 6

7. Daily Chore

----- 16

12. Live in the Moment

----- 26

3 Departure Announcement

----- 8

8. Self-Reflecting Room

----- 18

13. Self-Intro Album

----- 28

4. Travel Plan

----- 10

9. Favorite Place

----- 20

14. Own Way of Expressing

----- 30

5. Fellow Travelers

----- 12

10. Voice of Experience

----- 22

15. Gift of Words

----- 32

xi

WORDS FOR THE CARING

20. Disclosing Chat

----- 44

25. The Seen World

----- 54

30. Generational Mix

----- 64

16. Going Together

----- 36

21. Chance to Shine

----- 46

26. Personal Time

----- 56

31. The Amusement Committee

----- 66

17. Team Leader

----- 38

22. Preparation for the Dream

----- 48

27. Emotion Switch

----- 58

32. Hint of Feelings

----- 68

18. Family Expert

----- 40

23. Make it Funny

----- 50

28. Casual Counseling

----- 60

19. The Three Consultants
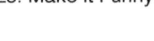
----- 42

24. Usual Talk

----- 52

29. Special Day

----- 62

WORDS FOR EVERYONE

33. Job-Specific Contributions

----- 72

34. On-the-Spot Helper

----- 74

35. Encouraging Supporter

----- 76

36. Personal Connections

----- 78

37. Mix-Up Event

----- 80

38. Inventing Jobs

----- 82

39. Delivering the Voice

----- 84

40. Warm Design

----- 86

xiii

About This Book

This book provides positive, practical hints for living well with dementia. Each hint describes a "context" that people with dementia and the people around experience and a "problem" that is commonly associated with the situation. Following this, a "solution" on how to cope with the problem is described.

These hints were determined through interviews, meaning that there are people are living well with dementia by using this knowledge. By sharing these wisdoms with a broad audience, our hope is to make everyone's life with dementia better.

As a distinctive feature of this book, each positive and practical piece of wisdom has been given an original name. For example, the hint that says to "create a place where the person with dementia can visit on their own, which the family also knows about" is titled "Favorite Place," and another that says to "make the cared person's room reflect them by filling it with the things that tell stories of moments from their life" is given the name "Self-Reflecting Room."

This way, the cared person and their family can think and talk about each hint as a distinct idea. For example, the family can have a conversation like "let's put this picture on the wall of his 'Self-Reflecting Room' so he can remember this family trip."

By including the words as a part of the family's vocabulary, these can be referred to as something to be considered within the family. The current problem that the word suggests can be worked on and solved and the potential risk of future problems can be reduced. We hope that Words for a Journey would collect the wisdom of all and contribute to a life well-lived with dementia.

How to Read

This book is a collection of 40 words that provide hints for living well with dementia. Each word is presented in a double-page spread. On the top of the left page in large print is the Word for the Journey. This word is more than just a label of the hint presented; it is a unique name that should become part of our vocabulary.

On the bottom of the left page, the "context" is described, followed by a "problem" that often occurs in that context. Even if you do not have the problem described at the moment, if the situation in the "context" matches you, the problem may likely occur in the near future.

Followed by the word "▼ Therefore," the "Solution" to the problem is stated. The solution is written in a rather abstract format, telling the reader what kind of an attitude or ways of thinking is needed to cope with the problem. Specific directions are not given, so you will need to decide how the solution would fit to your specific situation. After the word "▼ Consequently," the positive effects that the solution would bring are described.

The words in this book are categorized into three groups – "WORDS FOR THE CARED" (the person with dementia), "WORDS FOR THE CARING" (the patient's family), and "WORDS FOR EVERYONE" (society in general). Each group contains words that provide problems and solutions for the person in the corresponding group.

You can start by reading words from your own group, but do go ahead and take time to read the words from the other groups as well. You should be able to take a peek at the problems and hopes that people in the other groups might be feeling. That way you should become one step closer to helping people from all three groups to live well with dementia.

Please also note that in this book, all advice (i.e., "you might benefit from doing this") is written in the imperative form (i.e., "do this"). This is done so that the reader can look at the solution subjectively. The hints should not be something told to the reader as advice from a third person but something that the reader can consider firsthand.

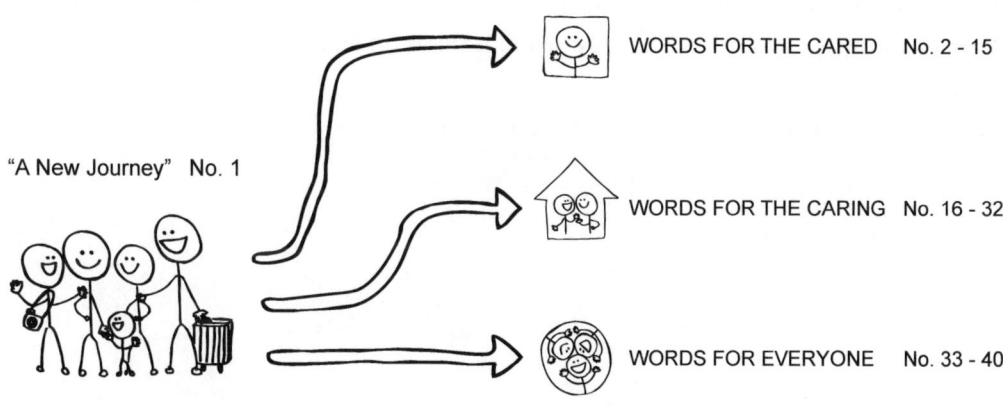

How to Use

There are two ways that the Words for a Journey in this book can be used. First, you can read through the collection of words and put those that you find interesting or useful into practice. Though each word is based on the experience of actual dementia patients and people close to them, there is no need to practice it in the same way. You can practice all or part of a hint based on how much it sympathizes with the pattern that you experience. This should become an opportunity for you to take a new action for positive change that you otherwise would not have taken.

The second way you can use the Words for a Journey is to use them as a part of your vocabulary to speak with other people about the hint that is described. You can talk about your own experience with one of the words to someone else or you can listen to their experience with the word. Conversations such as "Which word do you find most helpful?" "I think it is very important to give them a 'Chance to Shine'," "I don't quite get how to use 'Voice of Experience.' Could you tell me how you are doing it?" can be conducted. Through the talks, you may be able to gain new ideas from other people for applying the hints. In addition, using the Words for a Journey to talk out loud about your experiences will help you organize your thoughts, and other people would then be better able to understand and benefit from your experiences.

Be creative in using the Words for a Journey for living well with dementia.

Words For a Journey

1. A New Journey

WORDS FOR THE CARED	WORDS FOR THE CARING	WORDS FOR EVERYONE
2. The First Step	16. Going Together	33. Job-Specific Contributions
3. Departure Announcement	17. Team Leader	34. On-the-Spot Helper
4. Travel Plan	18. Family Expert	35. Encouraging Supporter
5. Fellow Travelers	19. The Three Consultants	36. Personal Connections
6. Can-Do List	20. Disclosing Chat	37. Mix-Up Event
7. Daily Chore	21. Chance to Shine	38. Inventing Jobs
8. Self-Reflecting Room	22. Preparation for the Dream	39. Delivering the Voice
9. Favorite Place	23. Make it Funny	40. Warm Design
10. Voice of Experience	24. Usual Talk	
11. Turning the Tide	25. The Seen World	
12. Live in the Moment	26. Personal Time	
13. Self-Intro Album	27. Emotion Switch	
14. Own Way of Expressing	28. Casual Counseling	
15. Gift of Words	29. Special Day	
	30. Generational Mix	
	31. The Amusement Committee	
	32. Hint of Feelings	

xix

WORDS FOR A JOURNEY

No.1

A New Journey

It is a new journey of living well with dementia.

You, a family member, or someone close to you has been diagnosed with dementia.

▼ In the context

At first, you may have trouble accepting the fact, from the fear that you may not be able to pursue the life plans that you previously had. Especially if it is your first time facing dementia, you will probably not know how to deal with it, and this can worsen your fears. Even if you do have prior experience caring for dementia patients, you might recall difficult memories from that time.

▼ Therefore

Accept the fact that you will have to make some changes in your life, and think of it as the start of a new journey. For example, because you will be spending more time together with your family, this will be a good opportunity to get to know them better. You will be going together to places where you used to go alone, and you will get a chance to reflect on each other's lives and notice things about them that you did not know before.

▼ Consequently

The time coming up is not a time for you and your family to lose what you already have, but rather one to recollect what you have missed and perhaps gain even more. How the family should spend this time is up to you and your family.

▷ 3. Departure Announcement   ▷ 16. Going Together   ▷ 33. Job-Specific Contributions

WORDS FOR THE CARED

 No.2

The First Step

Starting "A New Journey" of living with dementia.

You recently became aware of the possibility that you may have dementia.
You may have noticed that you have become more forgetful,
or people around you may have noticed symptoms.

▼ In this context

If you are reluctant to visit a doctor and do not receive proper care, it will hinder early detection and treatment and may cause your symptoms to worsen. No one likes to go to the hospital. What if you are diagnosed with dementia? What happens next? How should you tell your family? Many of these fears may make you even more reluctant to obtain medical care. However, not thinking about it will not make the disease go away; it will only lessen the chance for early treatment.

▼ Therefore

Think of your first visit for an examination as the start of a journey: a journey to live well, with others, as a strong individual. The examination should be viewed as the first step toward the future. Many people have dementia but still are living up to their full potential. You do not have to travel alone on this journey. Find family members who you feel comfortable with and can rely on and ask them to join you on the journey.

▼ Consequently

Knowing that you have dementia is a good thing, because you can get early and effective treatment. The fact that you took the first step of getting examined will strengthen your confidence. Facing dementia with such a positive attitude is said to impede the progress of the disease. This is the start. It should be a chance for you to consider what a good life means to you. Now, you can go ahead and make your **"Departure Announcement,"** create a **"Travel Plan,"** and recruit **"Fellow Travelers"** for the journey.

▷ 3. Departure Announcement   ▷ 4. Travel Plan   ▷ 5. Fellow Travelers

 No.3

Departure Announcement

Don't forget to tell people
you're going on the journey.

You are at the beginning of "**A New Journey**."

▼ In this context

Your family won't know how much they should get involved with your disease, especially if the symptoms are still light. If it progresses, your disease may advance without giving you and your family a chance to talk about how to face dementia as a family. Because you don't want to give your family extra worries, you pretend that nothing is wrong and try to solve everything yourself. Because your family is unaware of your diagnosis, they won't know when they should start caring for you. In this situation, preparation for care is delayed and may be insufficient to keep you safe.

▼ Therefore

Take the opportunity to tell your family about your disease. Announce that you have embarked on "A New Journey." Tell them that you might need their help. Ask them to join you on the journey as you face the disease together. Helping them understand your disease is important. Because it may be difficult to set up such an opportunity, the time immediately following diagnosis with dementia is the best time to do this.

▼ Consequently

Both you and your family can start to plan for your care. Once you make the first opportunity to talk about your diagnosis, it will become easier to talk about it again as the need arises. Only a short discussion is needed at first. Your family does not need to change everything all at once. You can continue to do what you can do on your own. After the first discussion, you and your family can start making your "**Travel Plan**" and recruiting "**Fellow Travelers.**"

▷ 4. Travel Plan 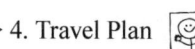   ▷ 5. Fellow Travelers   ▷ 16. Going Together

 No.4

Travel Plan

Creating the future together.

You have taken **"The First Step"** of your journey,
and made your **"Departure Announcement"** to your family.

▼ In this context

The life plans that you had before "A New Journey" may not work out exactly the way you planned after you have dementia. You may have a hard time coping with your disease, and some symptoms that limit your abilities may appear. Trying to face these difficulties alone can be stressful and hard. Because you are not going to live in solitude, keeping everything to yourself is unnecessary.

▼ Therefore

Get help from family, friends, and even specialists to rearrange a new life plan so that you can still live up to your full potential, even with dementia. Write out the things you want to do and the roles in which you want to take part. What kind of help do you need, and from whom, to accomplish those goals? Do not worry if you cannot think of your life plan right away. You can make your life plan and change it as needed with help from people around you.

▼ Consequently

By writing out a specific plan, you will become closer to actualizing it. You will start to believe that you can still accomplish anything on your journey. Your family and friends will probably help you accomplish these goals once they hear about them. Your journey with dementia is not going to be alone; you should make it with the help of people around you. Making your **"Travel Plan"** should become a good opportunity to realize this point.

▷ 5. Fellow Travelers   ▷ 22. Preparation for the Dream   ▷ 38. Inventing Jobs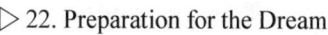

11

 No.5

Fellow Travelers

Having people beside you
should make you feel positive.

You have come to the beginning of "**A New Journey**,"
made your "**Departure Announcement**," and have made your "Travel Plan."

▼ In this context

Although you are carrying out your "Travel Plans," sometimes you may lose confidence in yourself and have a hard time cheering yourself up. Keeping up your confidence can be hard when you notice your memory becoming worse or you find yourself not being able to do things you were capable of before. When such things happen, you may tend to become blind to all the things you can still do. You can become depressed about your disability and lose the will to do anything else.

▼ Therefore

Find people that you can mutually empathize with and have fun with those people. For example, these may be old friends with whom who you share a common hobby. If some tasks are becoming difficult for you, these friends may be happy to help you once they understand your dementia. If you still wish to work or contribute to society, you can talk about it at a Family Association meeting. Carrying out your "Travel Plan" should not be something that you have to accomplish alone. Find good friends whose presence you can enjoy and share achievements together with.

▼ Consequently

With help from others, you will be able to accomplish goals that may be hard to do alone. What's more, it is great to have someone to share the joy of accomplishment with. Once you get the feeling that you can still do some things with the help of others, your confidence to try other things will grow. In addition, by increasing time spent with other people, the time you have to spend alone worrying will decrease, leading to a more fulfilled life.

▷ 4. Travel Plan    ▷ 17. Team Leader   ▷ 36. Personal Connections

13

 No.6

Can-Do List

Don't get too depressed by the things you can't do.

You are trying to live positively with dementia,
but there will still be times when you feel down.

▼ In this context

You may feel trapped by sad feelings caused by fright and worries about your future. Losing some of your abilities is a hard experience, and thinking that you might become more impaired is even harder. Because it may be hard for your family to notice small changes in you, it may seem that your family isn't taking these problems seriously. Stress from these things may cause you to feel down and keep your worries to yourself.

▼ Therefore

Make a list of the things that you can still do now. Take a pen and a piece of paper, and make the list as long as possible. The list can include activities from your everyday life, your hobby, or past work life. Talk to someone who can help you expand the list. Even the smallest things can go on the list.

▼ Consequently

You should notice that there is still a lot that you can do. Even small things that once were ordinary and nothing special will become special once you see them on the list. This long list should make you feel better, and a positive attitude toward yourself should return. You can use the items on this list to make your **"Daily Chore."**

▷ 7. Daily Chore    ▷ 12. Live in the Moment   ▷ 22. Preparation for the Dream

 No.7

Daily Chore

Even the smallest things matter
if you do them every day.

You increasingly need the help of other people to do things for you.

▼ In this context

If you start to think you shouldn't do something on your own and should have everything done by others, you will start to become unable to do even the tasks that you can do now. You might be worried about whether you can still do a task in the same way that you used to. On top of that, your family may offer to do everything for you out of concern. However, if you accept having everything done for you, your brain will receive less stimulation, and your symptoms may progress more rapidly.

▼ Therefore

Talk with your family and create a chore that you can do by yourself every day. It can be simple tasks such as watering a plant and giving the pet dog his food. Tasks such as folding the laundry and making coffee for the family… anything similar to this is important. Reference your **"Can-Do List"** to look for chores that you can do.

▼ Consequently

You can actively engage in the actions around your life. The chores will create a steady rhythm in your day, making it easier for you to maintain control over your life. The chores would also become a good starting point to have conversations with your family.

▷ 6. Can-Do List   ▷ 21. Chance to Shine   ▷ 38. Inventing Jobs

17

 No.8

Self-Reflecting Room

The things you like and the things you treasure
are what make you yourself.

You sometimes become afraid of gradually losing your memories.

▼ In this context

It is sad if in the near future, you cannot remember what things once composed your identity. When you become unable to do the things you used to do, it is natural to lose confidence and become worried. At such times, you might carelessly behave harshly with others. This would make you feel even more unlike yourself.

▼ Therefore

Make your room reflect yourself by filling it with the things you think are beautiful, the things that you treasure, and the things that tell stories about moments from your life. Photos of family and friends are a great place to start, and so are things such as letters, souvenirs, paintings, and collected items. Fill your desk and shelves with these items. Anything will do; have your room remind you of who you are.

▼ Consequently

You will be able to feel like yourself every time you enter your room. Your room will become a "mirror" that reflects your identity. Small details of memory may be lost, but it is the bits and pieces that together create the good feeling of being yourself. The items would also become a good conversation starter with people who visit your room.

▷ 13. Self-Intro Album    ▷ 14. Own Way of Expressing   ▷ 32. Hint of Feelings

 No.9

Favorite Place

A place outside the home,
which your family also knows about.

You have begun spending less time outside and more time inside your home.

▼ In this context

Staying inside your home all the time is not fun and may be tiring. No one likes to stay in the same place all the time. However, if you freely go out, your family may become worried that you may become confused and lost while you are out alone.

▼ Therefore

Find a place where you can go by yourself without any trouble, and make sure your family knows about the place too. If you already have such a place, tell your family that it is your "**Favorite Place**." If not, find a place such as a coffee shop or art museum near your home that you like, where you feel comfortable. You can ask a friend or a family member to help you find this place. Once you find your place, it would be nice to say hello to the people there so you can get on well early.

▼ Consequently

By having a second place besides your home where you can feel comfortable, you will be able to spend good times outside your home. Your family will feel comfortable letting you go out alone too if they know you are at your "**Favorite Place**." Even if a symptom of dementia occurs at the place, if the people there know about you, they would be able to treat you properly.

▷ 12. Live in the Moment   ▷ 34. On-the-Spot Helper   ▷ 36. Personal Connections

 No.10

Voice of Experience

Learn from people who've been through similar situations.

You have read and heard advice on living with dementia and are thinking of putting it into practice.

▼ In this context

In your head, you understand what you should do, but actually putting it into practice is hard. When and where should you start? How should you fit the advice to your own situation? Lack of details in the advice can make actual practice hard. Even if you do try, keeping up the practice may be hard because you are unsure whether you are doing it correctly.

▼ Therefore

Find a person who has been living with dementia and seek firsthand advice from them. If you already know such a person, you can go ahead and meet them. If not, you can look among your friends and other people on the Family Association for a person who could introduce you to someone. You can also find books written by people who are living well with dementia, and put yourself in their shoes while you read. You can even write to them or find out if they are holding lectures and go meet them.

▼ Consequently

By hearing personal stories of people in similar situations, you will be able to get a clearer image of how you could act. You can alter and fit their ideas to your life. Meeting these people and learning about their stories would become a source of confidence and should encourage you to do emulate them.

▷ 11. Turning the Tide   ▷ 18. Family Expert 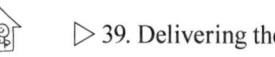   ▷ 39. Delivering the Voice

 No.11

Turning the Tide

Don't hold everything to yourself: share.

You are starting to get used to your journey of living well with dementia.

▼ In this context

You feel inconvenience in the environment around you and wish for that to change, but holding this discontent to yourself or within your family will not solve anything. What you and your family can solve alone is limited. Especially with regard to problems that require change in social systems or people's awareness, change is not easily achieved.

▼ Therefore

You can start by sharing your experience and discontent through media to make people become aware of the problems. You can set up a blog on the Internet or write to the editor's column in the newspaper about your troubles, experiences, and feelings about dementia. With help from the people around you, you can also set up a lecture to speak directly to people. You should work toward letting as many people as you can learn about your difficulties.

▼ Consequently

You can let people know what it feels like to have firsthand experience with dementia. Even if you could not think of a solution to the problems on your own, once people become aware of the difficulties, the stories may trigger ideas for solutions. Further, by preparing the stories and lectures, you will get a chance to organize your thoughts and experiences. In addition, this may provide you new people to connect with who you can help and encourage.

▷ 6. Can-Do List   ▷ 21. Chance to Shine   ▷ 39. Delivering the Voice

 No.12

Live in the Moment

Never forget how blessed you are
to feel happy in this moment.

A fun event such as a party or vacation is coming up.

▼ In this context

The event seems like fun, but somewhere in your mind you are hesitating to go. You may be scared that you might not be able to enjoy the event in the same way that everyone else does. You may be afraid that you will not be able to do the activity as you used to.

▼ Therefore

Jump into the event and enjoy the moment. Do not be worried about what you cannot do. If you keep on comparing your current self to your past self, you will never be able to enjoy anything. You should not compare yourself to others either. If you're afraid to go alone, have a family or a friend join you. Live in the moment and have some pure and honest fun.

▼ Consequently

You will be able to enjoy excitement that you usually would not experience. The fun you enjoy will become good motivation for going again next time. In addition, family and friends around you will also be happy to see you enjoying the event. Focus and live in each and every moment, and enjoy days filled with liveliness.

▷ 6. Can-Do List   ▷ 29. Special Day   ▷ 37. Mix-Up Event

 No.13

Self-Intro Album

A picture is worth a thousand words.

You recently have many opportunities to meet new people.

▼ In this context

You sometimes have trouble introducing yourself with words. You notice yourself taking more time putting yourself into words. Or you may notice the person having trouble understanding your words. It is not unusual to have trouble remembering things about yourself on the spot. This might cause you a small panic, making the situation worse. If such situations occur multiple times, you might become afraid to meet new people again.

▼ Therefore

Keep a small item with you, such as an album, which you can use to show who you are. The album can contain pictures of your family, your work, and your hobby, for example. It can be anything related to you or your past: magazine clippings, favorite sayings…. When you meet someone new, you can show them the album to introduce and talk about yourself. Spend time with your family and friends to create the album together.

▼ Consequently

This will basically become your portable "**Self-Reflecting Room.**" With it, you can stay calm and easily introduce yourself to others. Better yet, the pictures and items in your "**Self-Intro Album**" will make your introduction more attractive and interesting. New conversations can start from the items in the album too. In addition, creating the album itself will become a fun and valuable time to reflect on yourself and your life. If you create it with your family and friends, even better.

▷ 8. Self-Reflecting Room   ▷ 30. Generational Mix   ▷ 37. Mix-Up Event

 No.14

Own Way of Expressing

Anyone can be an artist.

You feel you are having trouble expressing your thoughts and emotions with words.

▼ In this context

Having trouble expressing yourself and not being understood is stressful and takes away from your confidence. It is tough to have trouble using words, especially when everyone around you is communicating with words. Because other people may not understand your troubles, you might tend to hold your stress within. If this continues, you may start to feel afraid to speak with people.

▼ Therefore

Find a way that you could enjoy expressing yourself that doesn't use words. If you like to take photos, you can collect photos of things you feel attracted to and express yourself through them. There are also people with dementia who draw pictures or create art. Wearing your favorite clothes or singing songs are also great ways to express yourself. If you are a funny person, you can even tell jokes to make everyone laugh.

▼ Consequently

You will remember how fun it is to express yourself, and you will gradually regain your confidence. Through focusing on your activity and creating things, your life will become even more fulfilling. If you collect your artwork, you can organize a local exhibition to display your work. Show your artistic sense and live a fun and colorful life!

▷ 8. Self-Reflecting Room   ▷ 13. Self-Intro Album 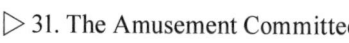 ▷ 31. The Amusement Committee

 No.15

Gift of Words

A "Thank You" is a great gift to give.

You are gaining support from many people around you.

▼ In this context

You are feeling thankfulness toward these people, but they will not understand if it is just in your mind. Even if you try to show thankfulness through your attitude, it may not be communicated or may be misunderstood. Especially if this involves someone very close to you, you may feel you do not have to say anything to them. However, when everyone is giving their best day by day, eventually your family and friends will get tired. In such a situation, not giving thanks for their efforts is sad.

▼ Therefore

Express your thankfulness in words. Close your eyes and think of the people that you are thankful for. Then, go meet and thank them. It does not need to be a special event. When someone does something for you, say thank you to them immediately. If you feel shy, you can write a short thank you note and hand it to them. There is no limit to the number of times you can say thanks to a person. They deserve it.

▼ Consequently

You can express your gratitude for the support from the people around you. This will create a warm a caring atmosphere, and everyone will become happy. By keeping thankfulness in your mind, you will start to see the effort that people are giving toward you that you did not notice before. It is this **"Gift of Words"** that create the bond between you and your "Fellow Travelers."

▷ 5. Fellow Travelers 　　▷ 16. Going Together 　　▷ 36. Personal Connections

WORDS FOR THE CARING

 No.16

Going Together

Taking the first step together.

You recently became aware, due to forgetfulness or other behavior, that a family member may have dementia.

▼ In this context

If you do not take them to the doctor to receive proper care, it will hinder early detection and treatment and may cause symptoms to worsen. You may feel bad suggesting that they go see the doctor, or the person might be unwilling to go. No one likes to go to the hospital. Especially with dementia, the fear of being diagnosed with it and not knowing what would happen next would make it even worse. However, not thinking about it will not make the disease go away but will only take away from the chances of early treatment.

▼ Therefore

Think of the first visit for examination as a start of "A New Journey" to live well with others as a strong individual with dementia and help them by taking the first step with them. The examination should become the first step for the future. Many people have dementia but are still living up to their full potential. However, for your loved family member, this would be a very frightening event. Stay beside them as they take the first step, and be there when they need you.

▼ Consequently

You will be able to provide your family with early care and proper treatment for the disease. This is the start. This should become an opportunity for the family to talk about what a good life means. If a family member gets diagnosed with dementia, you should appoint a **"Team Leader,"** and find **"The Three Consultants"** that you can rely on.

▷ 2. The First Step   ▷ 17. Team Leader   ▷ 19. The Three Consultants

37

 No.17

Team Leader

Don't hold everything to yourself.

You are going to be the closest person to support the family member with dementia.

▼ In this context

Trying to do everything by yourself is very stressful and tiring. Even if you think you can do it at the beginning, as the actual journey begins and as symptoms of dementia progress, the family member will start to require more support. Taking on all of this responsibility is hard work and sometimes even requires expertise. Before you know it, you will be overworking yourself.

▼ Therefore

Name yourself as the "leader" of the support team and determine who will be on the team and how the team will be organized. First of all, everyone in your family is a member of your team. Doctors and caretakers with expert knowledge who are helping you are also on the team. The leader of the team should talk with team members and see how each person can help. With this in mind, you should work on caring for your loved person as a team. Never try to do it all by yourself.

▼ Consequently

You will no longer have to be worried and stressed by yourself. With many members, the number of hands on the team will increase, and the number of brains will also increase. Ideas and information that you would not have thought of alone will come up. You can ask experts or people at the Family Association for ideas too. As a team, you will be able to address problems quickly. As a result, you will be able to stay calm and relaxed, making your "**A New Journey**" enjoyable and irreplaceable.

▷ 5. Fellow Travelers   ▷ 18. Family Expert   ▷ 19. The Three Consultants

 No.18

Family Expert

What happens at home, family members know best.

You have been collecting information about dementia care from books and the Internet.

▼ In this context

There is no guarantee that all of the information will work perfectly for your situation. It is rare that the information you find is talking about the exact same situation as the situation in your house. Many factors, such as the type of dementia, its progress, the personality of the person with dementia, and other family issues, will determine the best action to take. Therefore, just collecting information and putting it into action may not have the desired effect; it may even have detrimental effect.

▼ Therefore

Become an expert in the house that searches for and collects information that would be helpful specifically at your home. You may not be a dementia expert, but you are an expert about your family. Even if a book or a website says that something will work out "in general," you must stop and think if the information will work out specifically for your family. It is similar to raising a child: nothing goes exactly the way you hear it.

▼ Consequently

You will be able to follow the best practice for your family. You should have less stress from things not working out as they are supposed to. By making choices that work for your family, you will find an original path in your journey. By taking this approach toward information, you will be able to make changes and even think of original methods that can work. When other families also caring for a person with dementia consult you for help, you will be able to give them original advice on what worked.

▷ 6. Can-Do List   ▷ 17. Team Leader 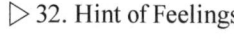   ▷ 32. Hint of Feelings

 No.19

The Three Consultants

Medical professionals, caregivers, and your friend:
the three connections you will need.

You have started providing care for your family member with dementia and are facing numerous problems.

▼ In this context

The problems are spread across a broad range of areas from daily life to expert knowledge, and it is difficult to find the right person to ask for help. For example, if you need expert help about medical or caregiving issues, you can consult a doctor. However, these people do not know much about your family and may not be able to give precise advice. On the other hand, your friends may know your family well, but they do not have expert knowledge.

▼ Therefore

Select three different types of consultants according to their expertise: medical help, caregiving help, and family help. Speak with the corresponding consultant based on the type of problem. The first type of consultants are doctors and care managers. You can ask them for expert advice on medical conditions and treatment. The second are your fellow caregivers, who also are caring for the family member with dementia. You can share and consult each other on the problems of caregiving. You can also share caregiving tips that you have found useful. The third group of consultants includes your friends who are not involved in caregiving. With them, you can talk about anything that friends share. These are the three connections you should have.

▼ Consequently

You will always have someone that you can talk to no matter the type of problem or difficulty you face. The fact you have someone you can consult should relieve some of your anxiety about caregiving. The sense of security gained from this by caregivers should bring a rich and comfortable time to the whole family.

▷ 17. Team Leader   ▷ 26. Personal Time    ▷ 35. Encouraging Supporter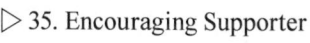

 No.20

Disclosing Chat

In between casual chats.

You haven't got the chance to tell the people around you
that a family member of yours has been diagnosed with dementia.

▼ In this context

If people around you do not know about the situation, you will not be able to ask for help, nor would they be able to help you. When is the best time to talk to your neighbors about the situation? It is especially hard to discuss dementia because people have a general image of dementia patients as wandering around and causing trouble for their neighbors. As time passes, disclosure becomes more and more difficult.

▼ Therefore

Do not set a special occasion to disclose the disease, but mention it casually during brief conversations with the person. It can be when you meet them at the supermarket or while you are walking the dog. You can disclose while raking leaves or commuting to work: any place you would have a casual conversation. The casualness is what makes it easier for you to disclose. After disclosing, let them know that you might need help from them in the future. There is no need to develop this into a deep conversation; keep it short and natural.

▼ Consequently

You will gradually gain supporters who you can ask for help. Some might be able to provide you with information or give you friendly help. Of course, some people who have prejudiced views on dementia. Turn away from their comments and refuse to be hurt by their words; focus on the people who are understanding. Build your support team in this manner.

▷ 17. Team Leader   ▷ 19. The Three Consultants   ▷ 35. Encouraging Supporter

 No.21

Chance to Shine

Small contributions matter.

You are putting effort into caregiving.

▼ In this context

If you do everything for the cared person, including the tasks that they can do on their own, eventually they would become unable to do anything. Caregiving does not mean living their life and doing everything for them. If you take away even the tasks that they can do on their own, they will receive less and less stimuli, and both their mind and body will weaken. They may still have the will and desire to help themselves but may keep quiet from the fear of causing trouble in the family.

▼ Therefore

Provide small opportunities for the cared person to contribute to the family. It can be something small, such as "could you grab the remote for me?" Providing the opportunity for small accomplishments would nurture a positive attitude in the cared person. This does not have to be limited to inside the house; you can give them a **"Chance to Shine"** even when other people are around.

▼ Consequently

The cared person can engage actively in their life. Working together to achieve a task will create positive and rich time spent together as a family. Further, by creating **"Chances to Shine"** outside the house, the cared person will be able to continue to contribute to and be accepted by the society.

▷ 7. Daily Chore   ▷ 32. Hint of Feelings   ▷ 38. Inventing Jobs

47

 No.22

Preparation for the Dream

A quick first action becomes
the shortcut to actualization.

You have found out that the person you are caring for
has a dream or goal that they wish to achieve.

▼ In this context

You want to help achieve their goals, but you think you should wait until they recover a little before they start. This might increase the possibility of never meeting the goal. Moreover, you may feel overwhelmed by caregiving. If their dream or goal requires some amount of preparation and effort, you might think it is not possible at the moment. As a result, you tend to put it off until later until it becomes too late.

▼ Therefore

Even if the goal seems hard to achieve, start now and move little by little toward its actualization. For example, if the person with dementia wishes to go on a trip to a place, you can start by looking for transportation and possible helpers who could assist on the trip. You can ask doctors and specialists for advice on how to prepare. One dementia patient had his family help him achieve the goal of climbing Mt. Fuji. If you prepare even a little every day, the possibility of achieving the goal will increase greatly.

▼ Consequently

You will be able to help the person who you are caring for actualize their dream. The act of helping them reach their goals itself would nurture a positive attitude in the cared person. It is passion and dreams that motivate a person from their heart. By preparing for their dream, you will be able to meet new people who will help you. Once your family does achieve the goal, it will nurture a significant feeling of achievement and passion for the next challenge.

▷ 4. Travel Plan    ▷ 17. Team Leader   ▷ 33. Job-Specific Contributions

 No.23

Make it Funny

Even the slightest things can seem funny.

You are giving care to your loved family member.

▼ In this context

When caregiving continues for a long period, topics of conversations tend to be centered around the disease itself and its care. Less time is spent enjoying fun conversations and laughing together. Such conversations are often serious and require precise communication of information. As a result, it becomes difficult to enjoy time spent together.

▼ Therefore

Pick up signs of enjoyment in their words, and reply to it to amplify their fun feelings. To make the time you spend together a pleasurable time, make the conversation as cheerful and funny as possible. To do so, look into the words they are speaking and pick up specific topics that they seem to enjoy. When doing so, you can exaggerate the fun to some extent. If you can lead the conversation in a fun direction, a warm atmosphere where you can trade jokes will eventually develop.

▼ Consequently

The days you spend with your family will become filled with laughter and smiles. The fun atmosphere should balance out the serious conversations that you must have. Such an atmosphere should relieve some of the stress of caregiving and create a positive attitude in family members. By picking up the person's words and making it funny and enjoyable for everyone, you are accepting who they are and highlighting their best qualities. Through this, strong family bonds are created.

▷ 12. Live in the Moment   ▷ 16. Going Together   ▷ 24. Usual Talk

 No.24

Usual Talk

Conversations that are the same as always.

You talk to your loved family member,
but sometimes they space out and you do not get an answer.

▼ In this context

If you decide they would not understand this topic and end the conversation, eventually you will have less and less to talk about with them. Talking to someone and not receiving a response is not a pleasant experience. However, if you stop the conversation there, only an awkward silence will remain during the precious time you spend together.

▼ Therefore

Continue the conversation even if they do not understand you and you do not receive an answer. If you do not get an answer, just continue talking to yourself. For example, if you have started the conversation "What should we do for Halloween this year?" and they do not respond, you can go ahead and continue, "I guess I will put out the gigantic scarecrow as we did last year." When doing so, try imagining how they would have had answered.

▼ Consequently

You will not have to choose and decide if you should say something to them every time something comes up to your mind. You can just go ahead and say it as you would have before. If they are in good condition, they might answer normally. Besides, starting a conversation and pretending you were just talking to yourself is something we usually do when we do not get a response. The most important thing is to take the effort to communicate to them.

▷ 5. Fellow Travelers   ▷ 16. Going Together   ▷ 23. Make it Funny

 No.25

The Seen World

Stand by them and share what they see.

Your loved person with dementia sometimes says things that differ from the facts and reality.

▼ In this context

Just plain neglect of what they are seeing will hurt the person's feelings. On the other hand, pretending that you see the same thing would be lying to them and that will not feel good. If your loved person fears something that is not there, denying this will not soothe their fright. If you keep neglecting what they are seeing, they will eventually become unable to believe in themselves. However, telling lies just to overcome the situation will have a negative effect on your trust.

▼ Therefore

Do not affirm or deny what they are saying or feeling. Accept their words as their seen world and act so that you can change what they are seeing. For example, they might say, "there's a little man standing on the table." If this happens, you should not say "Really! I see him, too!" nor should you say, "No, there is nothing on the table." First, accept their seen world: "There's a man standing on the table?" and see if you can steer their seen world back to normal: "Where is he? I'll get rid of him."

▼ Consequently

You can remain with them when they are experiencing fear from the hallucinations and attack the situation together. The most important thing is to stay next to them in their seen world to soothe their anxiety.

▷ 5. Fellow Travelers   ▷ 16. Going Together   ▷ 32. Hint of Feelings

55

 No.26

Personal Time

Time you spend on yourself
becomes a source of smiles for others.

You are spending much of your time giving care for your diagnosed family member.

▼ In this context

If you become too devoted to caregiving, you will eventually become emotionally tired and lose yourself in busyness. Taking a break, talking to your friends, and refreshing your mind and body are very important. However, as you get preoccupied with the caregiving, you may put off personal plans until later. Therefore, you will be left with less time for yourself, and even when you get the chance, you feel bad taking time off and cannot enjoy it to the fullest.

▼ Therefore

Gain cooperation from the people around you and take time off for yourself. For example, you can talk to the person you are caring for and their care managers to see if the family can take advantage of nursing homes. That way you can take longer amounts of time off that you can spend for yourself. You can spend this time on your hobby, with your friends, in taking a small trip, or to simply relax at home in order to refresh.

▼ Consequently

Your stress will be gone and you can start feeling refreshed once you return. If people see how refreshed and positive you are once you return, they will understand how important your **"Personal Time"** is. In the end, your **"Personal Time"** is not only good for yourself; By allowing you to recharge your energy, people around you will become positive too. After all, "living well with dementia" won't be accomplished unless everyone in the family can live well, right?

▷ 17. Team Leader   ▷ 27. Emotion Switch 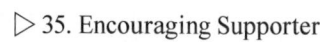   ▷ 35. Encouraging Supporter

 No.27

Emotion Switch

Don't get carried away by sudden emotions.

Even if you have the deepest love toward them, when giving care for the person with dementia, there will come times you feel frustration or anger.

▼ In this context

If these negative emotions pile up, one day it may explode. Negative emotions that you suppress in your mind will rarely be relieved. It is unusual that someone from outside the home will decide to help you spontaneously.

▼ Therefore

Have a way to switch your emotions and move on. For example, if you get into a fight, you can promise yourself that you will make up with them at the 3 PM coffee break. Make some nice coffee and bring it to them as a sign of reconciliation. When something happens that upsets you intensely, tell yourself that you can feel really depressed for the next 15 minutes, and then forget about it thereafter. Do something to distract yourself. It can be anything: listening to your favorite song, eating a piece of chocolate….

▼ Consequently

You will be able to cope with your emotions calmly. This will prevent damage caused by sudden fits to your relationship. You do not need to decide who was right and who was wrong. Take a step back and look at the situation calmly. This applies not just to caregiving but to any situation in life.

▷ 15. Gift of Words   ▷ 23. Make it Funny   ▷ 26. Personal Time

 No.28

Casual Counseling

Slip it in casually.

You are bearing most of the caregiving responsibility in the house.

▼ In this context

You are experiencing problems and worries that you try to handle by yourself and do not have the chance to talk about it to the rest of the family. You know everyone is busy, so you try solving everything by yourself. You can't talk about these problems in front of the person receiving care, so you have even a smaller chance to talk about it as a family. As a result, you start keeping the problems to yourself.

▼ Therefore

Find a casual opportunity to lightly disclose your feelings to family members. This can be during shopping, a short walk, in the car, or cooking, nothing serious. You don't need to sit and talk face to face with the person; it is probably done easier when facing the same direction. You can start by talking about all of the things you are doing for caregiving and about your feelings. If they are willing to listen, gradually disclose the distress you are experiencing. Don't demand anything from them, but rather simply tell them how you are feeling right now.

▼ Consequently

Your family members will get an idea of the kind of struggle you are going through. You don't have to demand anything from them at this point. It is up to them to decide how to react to what they hear from you. They might even be able to provide a solution, such as sharing the workload among the family.

▷ 17. Team Leader   ▷ 31. The Amusement Committee   ▷ 35. Encouraging Supporter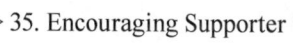

 No.29

Special Day

A day when you can be someone different
from your usual self.

The days are passing by and each day seems similar to the one before.

▼ In this context

When the days are monotonous, maintaining a positive feeling both for the caring and the cared is hard. Although you are lucky to be able to spend every day in peace, when life seems to be too similar every day, feeling happy can be difficult. This is especially true for the person being cared for because gradually they have less that they can do.

▼ Therefore

Set up a "Special Day" once in a while, where the person being cared can experience something different from the usual. For example, on their birthday, everyone in the family can dress up and eat out at a restaurant. You could also look for social events in town, such as a sporting event or a dance. For women, you can set up a day that they can visit a beauty parlor and enjoy dressing up and putting on makeup.

▼ Consequently

The **"Special Day"** will bring a special kind of excitement for everyone in the family. This special time spent together becomes an irreplaceable memory for everyone. You may be able to see some happy expressions or distinguished looks in the person that you usually don't see at home. You can easily ask for and gain cooperation from people around you because this is a "special" occasion. With these days sprinkled around the year, you can enjoy the journey as a family with a positive bright attitude.

▷ 12. Live in the Moment   ▷ 37. Mix-Up Event    ▷ 40. Warm Design

 No.30

Generational Mix

Have them meet a good mix of people.

The ones giving care are always the same few people.

▼ In this context

When the same people are always around, the cared person will be confined to a very small world. You may think people will lack understanding of dementia, so you tend to keep the person only around certain people who do understand the disease. However, for the person receiving care, who lacks the freedom to move around on their will, the few people around them mean the world to them.

▼ Therefore

Set up an opportunity for the cared person to meet and talk to children and adults of various generations. For example, you can invite children from the extended family. Children can supply ideas and excitement that adults cannot. One person with dementia was asked by her grandchild, "Grandma! Can you tell time?" The grandmother answers, "Yes, of course. I am an adult." This gave everyone at the place a smile. You can also invite young adults over to give them some advice on life.

▼ Consequently

Speaking with people from different generations will become a fun and inspiring experience. They may get stimulated by the young to take on some new challenges. For the visitors too, spending time with an elderly person will become a fresh and precious experience.

▷ 21. Chance to Shine   ▷ 29. Special Day   ▷ 37. Mix-Up Event

65

 No.31

The Amusement Committee

A fun event with family living far away.

Some family members are taking central roles in caregiving.

▼ In this context

Family and relatives who live far away rarely get a chance to spend time with the cared person. You think of traveling to go meet them, but you are not sure when and how you should take the cared person to go visit.

▼ Therefore

Set up a fun event and get different people from family and relatives involved in planning it. Contact family and relatives who live far away and invite them to plan the event with you. They can come visit or send a surprise gift for the cared person. They can even create an album or film a video of the person's favorite things as a present.

▼ Consequently

You can get people who usually are not involved in the caregiving to actively engage in planning fun for the cared person. In preparing for the special occasion, you can talk to them about the caregiving situation in a natural manner, because the information is necessary in planning what to do for the person. Above all, planning a surprise to make someone happy is a fun and nice thing to do. It will give you an opportunity to spend time together with extended family on something not directly related to caregiving.

▷ 12. Live in the Moment   ▷ 28. Casual Counseling   ▷ 29. Special Day

67

 No.32

Hint of Feelings

Searching for small hints of emotion
hidden in words and behavior.

You are starting to get used to giving care to your loved family member
diagnosed with dementia.

▼ In this context

When you are busy giving care for the person, you may be unknowingly making them do things against their will. Once you get used to the caregiving procedure, some tasks will start to be done on autopilot. When that happens, you sometimes overlook certain important signals and act without thinking much. This may result in doing things that the cared person does not want.

▼ Therefore

Look into the actions and words of the person you are caring for and search for hints of what they truly want. If you focus on them carefully, you might find out what they value. For example, they may make some sarcastic remarks, but on the inside, they might be concealing distress or desires. If certain words or actions catch your mind, you can ask them about it. It may uncover hidden fears or discontent.

▼ Consequently

You can give what they truly need. By understanding their emotions at a deeper level, you can create a more intimate relationship. Even if they have trouble expressing their emotions, you can assist them by detecting small signals from their behavior. Then, you will be able to truly live well together, fulfilled with small bits of happiness.

▷ 14. Own Way of Expressing   ▷ 15. Gift of Words   ▷ 16. Going Together

WORDS FOR EVERYONE

 No.33

Job-Specific Contributions

What can I do to help?

Approximately eight million people are believed to have dementia today, including potential patients, in Japan alone. One in four elderly have either dementia or are showing early symptoms of the disease.

▼ In this context

Though the people with dementia need help in a wide variety of areas in their daily life, little effort is made to provide assistance outside the medical and welfare fields. Though many adults have pride in the work they do, very little have thought of the connection between their work and dementia. Dementia is an issue that we need to tackle as a society, but very few of us know what we can specifically do to help with the problem.

▼ Therefore

Set an opportunity to think about how you can help with the issue if dementia in your work, and put the ideas into practice. For example, you can work to set up a slow lane at the supermarket where the customer can take their time to pay for merchandise or you can train yourself to know what to do when you meet a dementia patient on the bus who needs help. You can assemble others at your workplace who have similar concerns about dementia and discuss how your workplace can help out in the issue. You can also create an opportunity to actually meet dementia patients and their families to learn about the difficulties they are facing and see what other people from different fields are doing at their companies to ameliorate the situation. Sharing information will start a community, and a community will start change.

▼ Consequently

You might find ideas for new goods and service that would help people who are struggling with dementia. If you form a community concerning dementia at your workplace, it will deepen your understanding of the disease, and the topic can spread throughout the company and subsequently throughout society. By facing the fact that many of us are or will be diagnosed with dementia, you will be able to gain a broader viewpoint to think about customer service; ultimately, a better caring and competitive organization that cares about the important issue will be born.

▷ 11. Turning the Tide   ▷ 22. Preparation for the Dream   ▷ 38. Inventing Jobs

 No.34

On-the-Spot Helper

Helping out a little, in a small amount of time.

You are walking in town and see someone showing unusual behavior.
They may be walking in an uncoordinated manner
or having trouble controlling a machine.

▼ In this context

That person might have dementia and may need help. Leaving them alone might lead to accidents and danger, or the person might need help for a very long time. Symptoms of dementia may cause the person to become confused about their situation, making it difficult for them to stay calm and ask for help. Although you may want to help, you may not know what exactly to do, or you might be in a hurry and not have the time to help.

▼ Therefore

Become an "On-the-Spot Helper" for a short amount of time, and offer to help. Tell them that it is dangerous to walk outside the sidewalk and take them to a safer place. If they are having trouble operating a ticketing machine, you can offer to help them buy the tickets. If you are in a real hurry and cannot help out directly, you can alert someone who is qualified to help, such as station staff, that there is someone who needs assistance.

▼ Consequently

Many accidents and trouble can be prevented. It may require courage at first to speak to the person, but as you accumulate experience as an **"On-the-Spot Helper,"** such actions would become more natural. Eventually, you might become motivated to learn more about dementia.

▷ 9. Favorite Place    ▷ 25. The Seen World   ▷ 33. Job-Specific Contributions

 No.35

Encouraging Supporter

Watch over and assist.

You have a friend who is giving care to a family member with dementia.

▼ In this context

You feel rude to step into family problems, so you do not touch on the topic. As a result, families holding the person with dementia become more and more isolated. If you don't know much about the disease, you tend to hesitate to ask about the topic since you are not sure if you can be any help. The patient and the family are hesitant to ask for help because they do not want to cause any trouble to you.

▼ Therefore

Have them talk about their situation and what kinds of efforts they are putting in. Listen, understand their efforts and offer some support. Do not be afraid if you might not be much help. You can start by listening to their story. Once you start to understand their situation, become their "**Encouraging Supporter**." Nothing hard. All you have to do is to stay by them and provide words of encouragement. "Good work! He must be very happy with a good caregiver" "You look tired! Make sure you get good rest, okay?" These words of encouragement mean a lot to them and should cheer them up.

▼ Consequently

Having an understanding supporter will become great relief for your friend, especially because they are apt to easily become isolated from other people. Even if you do not have any specific knowledge about dementia, you can still be a big help. By becoming an "**Encouraging Supporter**" and watching them give care, you can learn about caregiving too for when the need arises in your family.

▷ 19. The Three Consultants   ▷ 28. Casual Counseling   ▷ 26. Personal Time

77

 No.36

Personal Connections

Learning from friends.

You are seeking for ways to learn more about dementia and get involved.

▼ In this context

Starting by reading books or taking classes on dementia and caregiving is overwhelming and hard to continue. Dementia is just a general term for the disease, and so if you try to learn all about it, you will soon find out how much more there is to it. Because there are different types of dementia, such as Alzheimer's or Lewy bodies, symptoms and care will vary based on progression of the disease. Just learning about these facts without an actual knowledge of specific approaches to caregiving will be pointless.

▼ Therefore

Create a connection with an actual patient, and learn necessary information by spending time with them. You can join an event where dementia patients participate, and look for connections there. Once you become friends with them, you will start to notice the knowledge and skills you need to understand them. Through spending time and talking with them, you will naturally learn how to support them.

▼ Consequently

You can learn specific and practical knowledge on living well with dementia. Through spending time with an actual patient you will start to see the kinds of problems that the society holds that needs to be solved. For the patient and their family too, this connection will open up their circle of support. There is no need to hesitate; you can start now.

▷ 5. Fellow Travelers   ▷ 9. Favorite Place 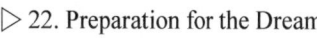   ▷ 22. Preparation for the Dream

 No.37

Mix-Up Event

Dementia-or-not, come enjoy with us!

You are planning an event for people with dementia and their family members.

▼ In this context

It is hard for participants to truly have fun at an event designed specifically for the people with dementia. Events that handicapped people can join are precious. However, if the organizers become too attentive of the dementia patients, the distinction between the patients and the others will become obvious. In such a situation, both sides will have a hard time enjoying the event comfortably.

▼ Therefore

Organize the event so that people can enjoy regardless of if they have dementia or not. Don't organize activities based on whether a task can be done by a dementia patient or not. Instead design activities that require participants to cooperate to achieve a common goal. Besides, symptoms of dementia differ from person to person due to their type and progress; so different tasks will be difficult for different people. You do not need to draw a concrete line to distinguish people; mix them all up in to one huge salad bow so that everyone can equally enjoy.

▼ Consequently

By designing the event so that people can enjoy no matter who they are, each person will be able to stand out. If everyone, even the organizers, are laughing and joking together, the time spent will become an important experience not only for the dementia patient and their family but also for the organizers. Take a lot of photos and share them online. As the number of such events increase, the society should become comfortable for people with dementia.

▷ 12. Live in the Moment   ▷ 13. Self-Intro Album   ▷ 29. Special Day

 No.38

Inventing Jobs

If no existing job fits them, just create a new one.

A dementia patient wishes to contribute to the society.

▼ In this context

Though the person may have the will to work, it is often difficult to find a job that they are capable of doing. Most jobs don't take into account the limitations and difficulties that dementia patients have. Therefore, when a person with dementia takes the position, negative parts such as tasks they can't do or have difficulty in doing tend to stand out. This will lead to diminishment of the person's confidence, since they will have a difficult time fitting into the given position.

▼ Therefore

Create a new opportunity to contribute to the society with the help from companies and local government. Consult with different people to create jobs that people with dementia can still do. There are already nursing homes and NPOs that are cooperating with companies to create new styles of work. Some research into these efforts may be helpful.

▼ Consequently

If the job is worthwhile doing for the dementia patient, it will create a nice accent to their life. This excitement cannot be experienced at home, and it will also extend their connections with other people. For those creating the new jobs, this could become a new model of working. When other companies see this and start doing the same, more jobs could be created.

▷ 7. Daily Chore   ▷ 21. Chance to Shine   ▷ 33. Job-Specific Contributions

83

 No.39

Delivering the Voice

If the word doesn't spread, nothing will change.

You regularly spend time with the people with dementia,
and often work together.

▼ In this context

There are still many people in the world who are unconcerned or uninformed about dementia. We are far from working as a society to attack the issue of dementia. For those who do not have family or friends with dementia, the disease is only something they see on the news. On top of that, the information they do hear is biased with problems about the disease, creating false preconceptions. Such a society is far from a society where people can live well with dementia.

▼ Therefore

Help deliver the voice of the people with dementia and their family to as many people as possible. For example, if there is going to be an event where a dementia patient is going to give a talk, you can spread the word so that more people will join the event. If you are developing a product or a service at your wok, you can invite dementia patients to talk about frustrations and comments they have about the product or service, to make it dementia-friendly. You can also establish cooperation from schools to have young students help spread information about dementia.

▼ Consequently

The voice of dementia patients and their family will be delivered to people they would not have been able to reach on their own. People will see you putting in effort for the cause, and do the same. You might be able to meet someone who can deliver the voice to an even broader audience. Ultimately, people in the region will start to become more familiar with dementia.

▷ 10. Voice of Experience 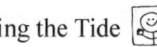   ▷ 11. Turning the Tide 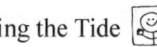   ▷ 36. Personal Connections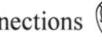

85

 No.40

Warm Design

Not cool. Not Hot.
Warm: comfortable and fits you.

Due to **"Job-Specific Contributions"**
you have thought of a new product or service
targeted for the people with dementia and the people around them.

▼ In this context

If you put all of your effort into its function and its design is unattractive, your target will not want to use it. Caregiving goods must be flexible and have multiple functions so that it can accommodate for many different circumstances. However if it has a bad design, people will have little interest in using it.

▼ Therefore

Make it so that the user feels the design fits them perfectly, and gives them a sense of kindness. It should not be just a cool, attractive design. Nor should it be a design that tracks hot trends. It should have a warm design that fits you perfectly and gives you a warm feeling in the heart. For example, if it is a daily commodity, make it a design that makes you feel happy when using it every day. If it is a bus for a nursing home, don't just paint it white with the name of the facility and some random pictures of children painted on it, but design the bus so that you feel proud to travel on it.

▼ Consequently

The objects and the places in your life will become a source of power for both the cared and the caring. Such a design will become an important contribution to living well with dementia. When "**Warm Design**" becomes more common, the people with dementia will start to get the freedom of choice among different designs across several companies, all offering warm design.

▷ 11. Turning the Tide   ▷ 12. Live in the Moment   ▷ 33. Job-Specific Contributions

The Journey Continues …

We are still searching for more "words for a journey" for living well with dementia. Some of you may have original "words for a journey" in mind. There should be even more "seeds" for possible new words in your daily life too.

If you have a feeling that you might have "words for a journey," please share it with someone. Write it out for that person. Create your original "words for a journey."

Further, please send us any of your wisdom to live well with dementia. It can be in the form of a Word for a Journey, or it can be just a story of your experience. We will continue our search for new "words for a journey" together with you readers in order to keep updating our collection of words.

The Words for a Journey Project
E-mail: journey@sfc.keio.ac.jp
Web-site: http://journey.sfc.keio.ac.jp/

Postal Address: Iba Laboratory, Keio University
Endo 5322, Fujisawa, Kanagawa 252-0882, Japan

Utilizing Words for a Journey: Ideas for Every Stakeholder

The goal of this book is for people with dementia and their families to gain insights on living well with dementia. This book enables people to absorb the words (hints) from Words for a Journey into their daily lives and engage with others to expand their understanding of the disorder.

This book is intended to be utilized not only by people with dementia and their families but also by wider audiences. This includes people in Family Associations, nonprofit organizations (NPOs), volunteers, care providers at medical and other facilities, people working for municipalities and other government agencies, educators, companies creating new products and services to make the world a better place, and even people who do not yet have firsthand experience with dementia. If you are one of these people, keep reading to find out how you can use this book.

[People involved with Family Associations, NPOs, and volunteers in the field]
You can hold discussions for participants to talk about their experiences with dementia. Pick two, three, or more words (hints) from the 40 words in this book and invite people to share their experiences with these words. For example, introduce the word "Favorite Place" at your Family Association and ask attendees if they have such a place and how they are using it. Their "Favorite Place" may be a local coffee shop or the library. Ask them why they call this place as their favorite and how their lives would be different if they didn't have this place. When listening to their peers' stories, the other participants will be able to envision their own "Favorite Place" and motivate them to find a place of their own if they don't already have one. The Words for a Journey will become a conversation starter to enable comfortable conversations even among people who do not yet know each other well.

[For people in caregiving and other medical fields]

You can create conversation opportunities for patients with dementia, their families, and other people who use your facility. In addition, your staff can engage in constructive conversations with these people to learn from each other and thus add value to the quality of the services provided. Words for a Journey is also useful when patients with dementia and their family members are experiencing a tough time. The words contained herein will help them view dementia in a more positive light. These hints that come from a nonprofessional point of view would become useful in a different way from the usual professional advice.

[For people working with municipalities and other government agencies]

You can use Words for a Journey to help you talk with people who have dementia and their families about how the government support can be improved. This will help you in sharing and communicating contexts and problems to have a constructive discussion.

[For educators]

Even if you do not have a personal experience with anyone having dementia, this book will give a good peek about how would it be to have the disease or someone close to you have the disease. For students at any level from elementary school to college, knowing better about the people who they share the same community with will become a good experience that will make them think more about their future, develop awareness for the issue, and nurture a caring attitude toward others.

[For industry leaders]

The problems and concerns people with dementia face should help you think about new products and services. Think beyond words such as "Warm Design." However, many words can become a good idea for a start. If every company were to take a role in resolving issues related to dementia, we would have a great foundation to work as society that "lives well with dementia."

Afterword

This book was born by the collaboration between Makoto Okada (Fujitsu Laboratories Ltd.) of the Dementia Friendly Japan Initiative, which works to connect people across borders from companies, municipalities, and NPOs to make society a better place for people living with dementia and Takashi Iba (Keio University) who studies and develops methods to enhance creativity. The 40 Words for a Journey in this book are based on the philosophy of a method called Pattern Languages.

Pattern Language was originally developed in the 1970s by architect Christopher Alexander. He called structures that appear in well-structured and lively forms of architecture as "patterns" and worked to capture and communicate these recurring structures as a "language" (with words).

His challenge was to create new words that could be understood by anyone so as to introduce novices into the architectural process of designing towns and houses that otherwise would require professional knowledge. He believed that true beauty and liveliness of architecture could only be achieved if the gap between the creator and the user was removed and the actual people who were to live in the towns and houses participated in their production so that they could continue improvement even after the architects left. What a lovely idea!

At the Iba laboratory of Keio University, students have been studying pattern languages for applying the method to design not just physical objects but also intangible human actions. Mr. Okada joined the lab and a project to scribe out the knowledge to "live well with dementia," which only a limited number of people had until that point, as a pattern language started. Thus, the world's first pattern language in the social welfare field was created. Pattern languages help us understand the knowledge inside the human mind for two reasons.

First, this knowledge is usually "fluid" inside the human mind and is shaped into the required form every time it is used. We need a new word (a container) to solidify the idea and make it communicable. The context, problem, and solution of the pattern format establish a good framework to capture the ambiguous knowledge inside one's mind.

Second, pattern languages enable us to communicate this captured knowledge to other people. Trying to communicate our thoughts is usually difficult, but the verbal expression of our ideas as words can be used to communicate our thoughts.

We will continue our support to make the lives of people associated with dementia better, and we encourage people regardless of their field to put their "positive and constructive ideas" into "words" to create a better world. Our hope is that the lives of everyone who picks up this book will be filled with joy and liveliness. Thank you.

Takashi Iba

Acknowledgements

This work would not have been not possible without the help of many major players. We especially acknowledge the following people for the help they provided creating this book, including interviews and feedback: Naomi Higuchi, Yoichiro Igarashi, Koji Inagaki, Mieko Inoue, Miyako Inoue, Sumio Iwanami, Yumiko Kahata, Kazuhiro Kameda, Takayuki Maeda, Akihiro Matsuura, Toshiko Matsuura, Kaori Nodera, Jun Sakurada, Masahiko Sato, Shinji Sudo, Kenzo Yamada, Shimpei Yamamoto, Tatsuya Wakano, People of the DFJI, and People of the RUN TOMO-RROW. In addition, we thank Kaori Harasawa for her help in creating the illustrations in this book.

We would like to thank to Richard Gabriel, Linda Rising, Joseph Yoder, Rebecca Wirfs-Brock, Jenny Quillien, Lise Hvatum, Bob Hanmer, Mary Lynn Manns, Christian Kohls, and Christian Köppe for encouraging our quest to create a new type of pattern language. Thank you!

References

Alexander, C. (1979) *The Timeless Way of Building*, Oxford University Press.

Alexander, C., Davis, H., Martinez, J. and Corner, D. (1985) *The Production of Houses*, Oxford University Press.

Alexander, C., Ishikawa, S., Silverstein, M., Jacobson, M., Fiksdahl-King, I. and Angel, S. (1977) *A Pattern Language: Towns, Buildings, Construction*, Oxford University Press.

Bryden, C. (2012) *Who will I be when I die?*, Jessica Kingsley Publishers.

Bryden, C. (2005) *Dancing with dementia*, Jessica Kingsley Publishers.

Nakamura, S. (2011) *Bokuga Mae wo Muite Aruku Riyu: Jiken, Pick Byo wo Kakaete Ima wo Ikiru [Why I can go on facing forward: Get Over Pick disease to live the moment]*, Chuohoki Publishing, 2011

Manns, M.L. and Rising, L. (2005) *Fearless Change: Patterns for Introducing New Ideas*, Addison-Wesley.

Ota, M. (2007) *My Way: Ninchisho to Akaruku Ikiru Watashi no Hoho [My Way: Being with Dementia positively]*, Shogakukan.

Sato, M. (2014) *Ninchisho ninatta Wtashiga Tsutaetaikoto [What I Want to Share, who Live with Dementia]*, Otsuki Shoten.

Pattern Language 3.0 Catalogue Series

Learning Patterns: A Pattern Language for Creative Learning
Takashi Iba *with* Iba Laboratory, 2014

Learning Patterns is a set of patterns that describe the secrets of creative learning. It offers 40 patterns, each of which captures an aspect of a good learning. Create opportunities for learning on your own by launching and implementing your own project, as well as learn by actively creating in collaboration with others!

Presentation Patterns: A Pattern Language for Creative Presentations
Takashi Iba *with* Iba Laboratory, 2014

Presentation Patterns is a set of patterns that describes the secrets of creative presentations. There are 34 patterns, each of which captures an aspect of a good presentation. Treat your presentation not as merely a chance to explain your idea, but as a chance for creation. Work with your audience to trigger new findings in them!

Collaboration Patterns: A Pattern Language for Creative Collaborations
Takashi Iba *with* Iba Laboratory, 2014

Collaboration Patterns is a set of patterns that describes the secrets of creative and collaborative project work. Each of the 34 patterns captures an aspect of a good collaboration. Create new values that can change the world by collectively producing an emergent synergy that cannot be reduced to any one team member, but can only come from developing the capacity to enhance each other!

Words for a Journey: The Art of Being with Dementia

Takashi Iba and Makoto Okada
with Iba Laboratory and Dementia Friendly Japan Initiative, 2015

Words for a Journey collects practical knowledge on living with dementia. Though many hold negative impressions of the disease, there are still many who are living well with dementia. This book collects wisdom and stories from such people, and extracts its essence to be shared widely.

Survival Language: A Pattern Language for Surviving Earthquakes

Tomoki Furukawazono and Takashi Iba
with Survival Language Project, 2015

Survival Language is a pattern language to improve survival rates when a catastrophic earthquake occurs. There are twenty patterns, each of which captures practices of Designing for Preparation, Designing for Emergency Action, and Designing for Life After a Quake that form patterns found in the many lessons Japan has learned from numerous earthquakes.

Change Making Patterns: A Pattern Language for Fostering Social Entrepreneurship

Eri Shimomukai and Sumire Nakamura
with Takashi Iba, 2014

Change Making Patterns is a set of patterns that describe the secrets for creating social change. There are 31 patterns, each of which captures the aspects of creatively solving social issues. Launch your own change-making project to tackle social issues in your own context to take part in creating a better world!

Authors

Takashi Iba is an associate professor in the Faculty of Policy Management and the Graduate School of Media and Governance at Keio University, Japan. He received a Ph.D. in Media and Governance from Keio University in 2003 and continued as a visiting scholar at the MIT Center for Collective Intelligence during the 2009 academic year. Collaborating with his students, Dr. Iba created many pattern languages concerning human actions. He authored *Learning Patterns* (2014), *Presentation Patterns* (2014), *Collaboration Patterns* (2014), and many academic books in Japanese such as the bestselling *Introduction to Complex Systems* (1998).

Makoto Okada is a Senior Manager in charge of Management of Technology (MOT) in the R&D Planning Office at Fujitsu Laboratories, Ltd. and a Researcher in the Research Center for Practical Wisdom, Fujitsu Research Institute. He is also a Visiting Research Fellow at the Center for Global Communications, International University of Japan, and on the Board of Directors for the Dementia Friendly Japan Initiative and on the Advisory Board of the Dementia Friendship Club.

Iba Laboratory is an innovative research lab at Keio University that creates pattern languages in various fields, including learning, presentation, and collaboration, to support creative acts of humans in a wide range of fields. The book Presentation Patterns received the "Good Design Award" in 2013.

Dementia Friendly Japan Initiative (DFJI) is a cross-sector network, which reassesses the issues related to dementia as an issue of social design. People from industries, municipalities, and NPOs share their knowledge to work experimentally toward a better future.

Contact Us:
The Words for a Journey Project
E-mail: journey@sfc.keio.ac.jp
Web-site: http://journey.sfc.keio.ac.jp/

Postal Address: Iba Laboratory, Keio University
Endo 5322, Fujisawa, Kanagawa 252-0882, Japan

Words For a Journey

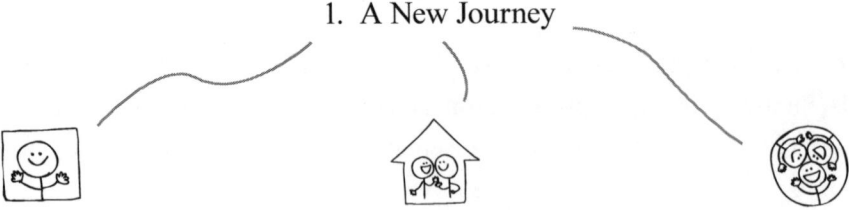

1. A New Journey

WORDS FOR THE CARED

2. The First Step
3. Departure Announcement
4. Travel Plan
5. Fellow Travelers
6. Can-Do List
7. Daily Chore
8. Self-Reflecting Room
9. Favorite Place
10. Voice of Experience
11. Turning the Tide
12. Live in the Moment
13. Self-Intro Album
14. Own Way of Expressing
15. Gift of Words

WORDS FOR THE CARING

16. Going Together
17. Team Leader
18. Family Expert
19. The Three Consultants
20. Disclosing Chat
21. Chance to Shine
22. Preparation for the Dream
23. Make it Funny
24. Usual Talk
25. The Seen World
26. Personal Time
27. Emotion Switch
28. Casual Counseling
29. Special Day
30. Generational Mix
31. The Amusement Committee
32. Hint of Feelings

WORDS FOR EVERYONE

33. Job-Specific Contributions
34. On-the-Spot Helper
35. Encouraging Supporter
36. Personal Connections
37. Mix-Up Event
38. Inventing Jobs
39. Delivering the Voice
40. Warm Design